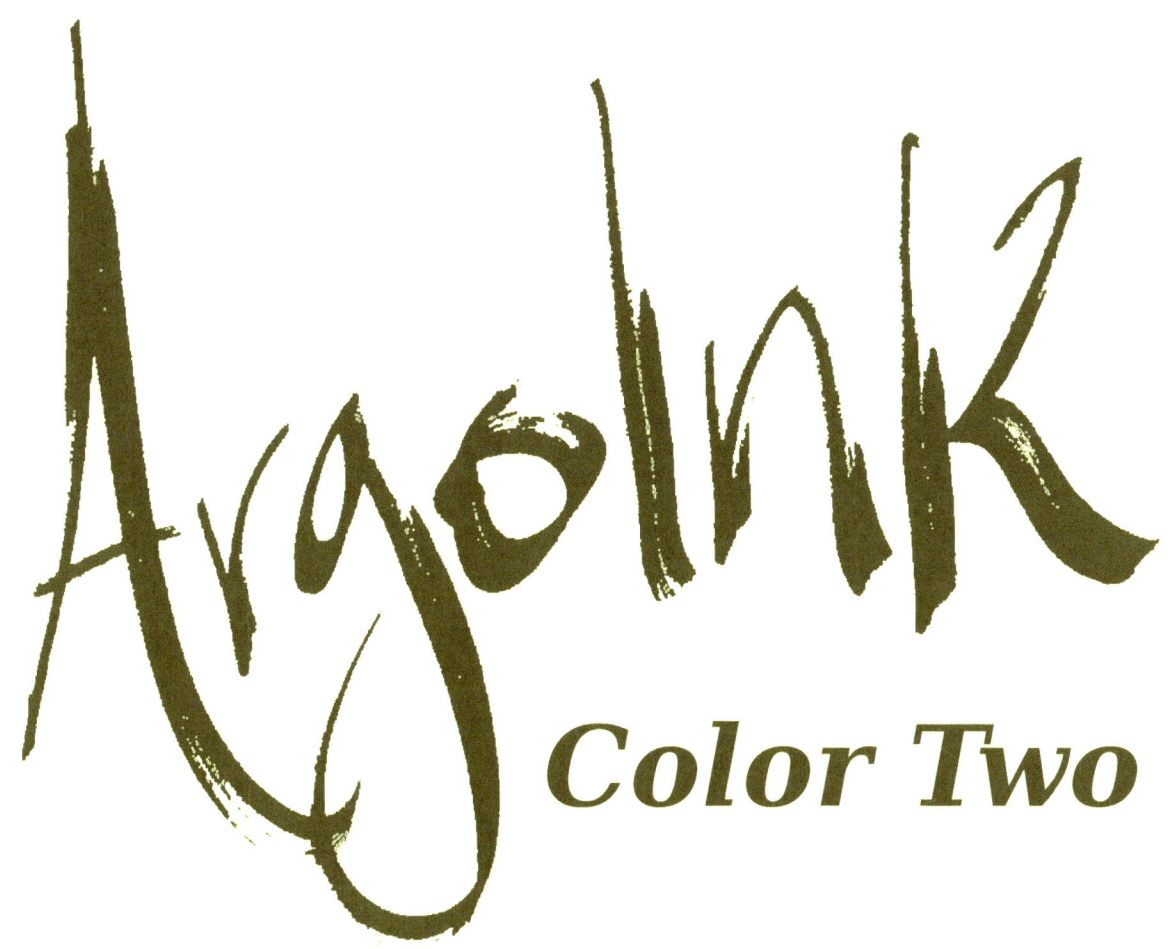

ArgoInk

Color Two

Illustrated by

Chris Argo

ISBN-13: 978-1475016352
ISBN-10: 1475016352

http://www.ArgoInk.com

To my beautiful wife

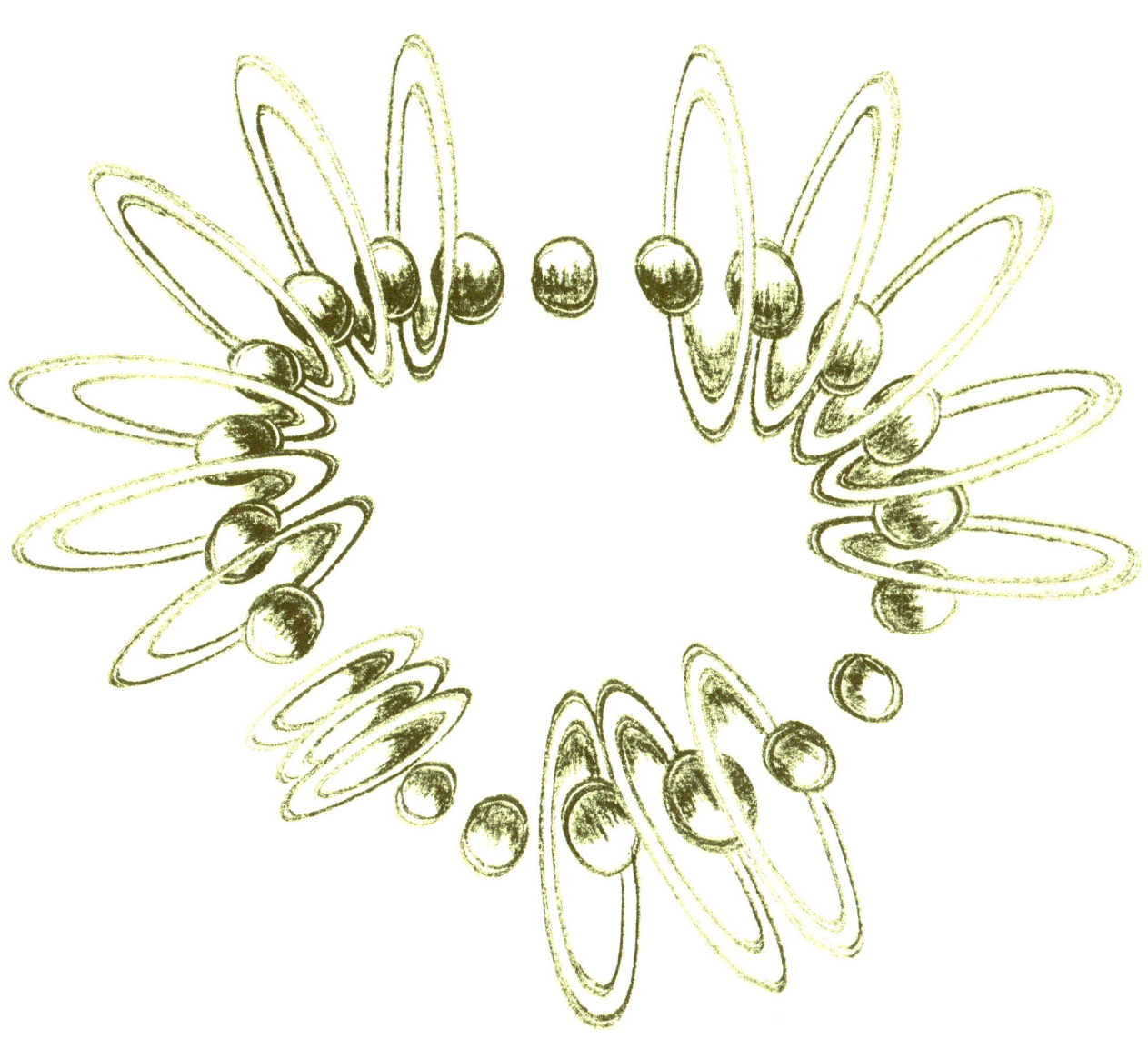

"Our deepest fear is not that we are inadequate. Our deepest fear is that we are powerful beyond measure. It is our light, not our darkness that most frightens us. We ask ourselves, who am I to be brilliant, gorgeous, talented, fabulous? Actually, who are you NOT to be? You are a child of God. Your playing small does not serve the world. There is nothing enlightened about shrinking so that other people won't feel insecure around you. We are all meant to shine, as children do. We were born to make manifest the glory of God that is within us. It's not just in some of us; it's in everyone. And as we let our own light shine, we unconsciously give other people permission to do the same. As we are liberated from our own fear, our presence automatically liberates others."

-- Nelson Mandela

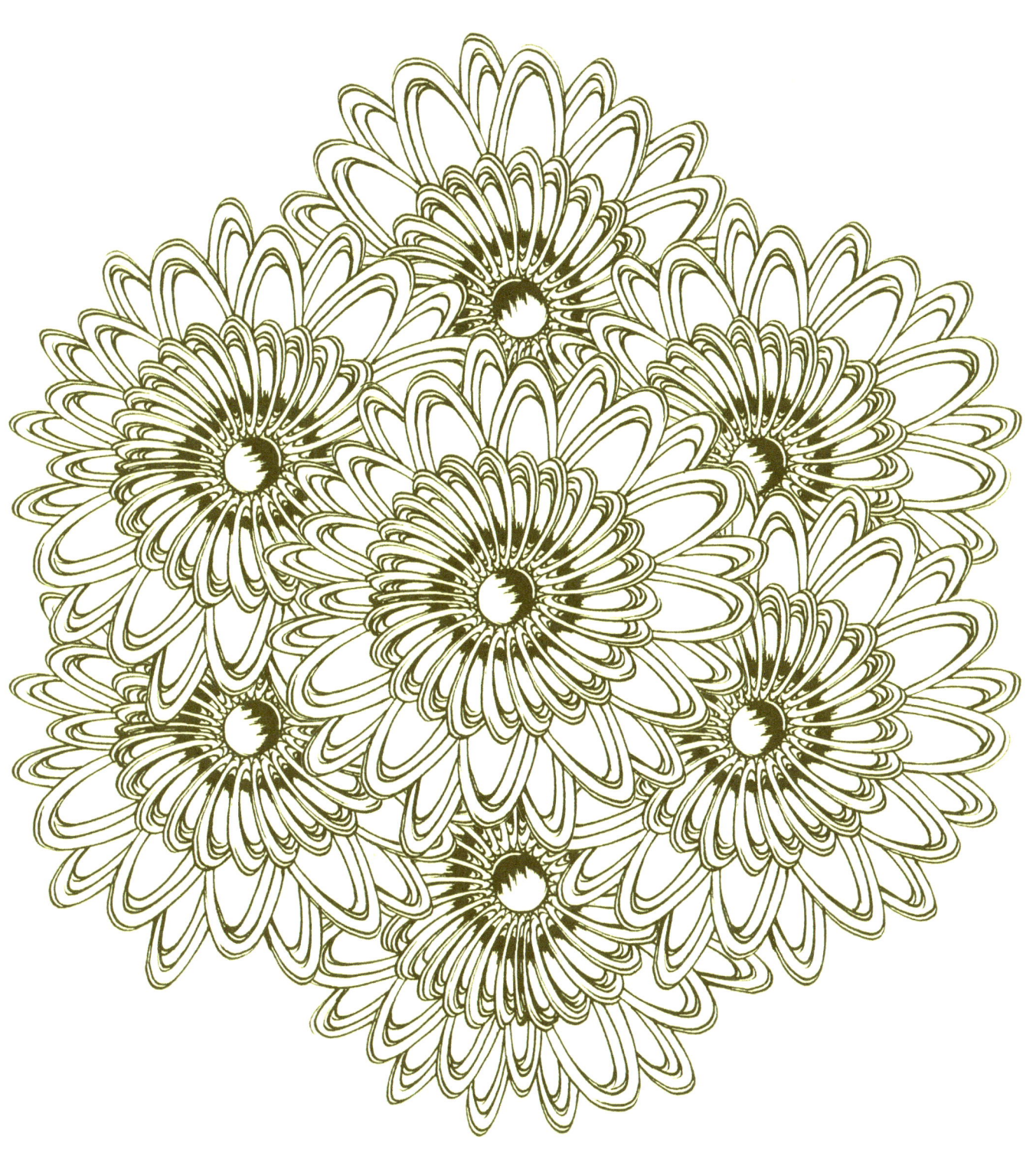

Pleasant it is, when over a great sea the winds trouble the waters, to gaze from shore upon another's great tribulation; not because any man's troubles are a delectable joy, but because to perceive you are free of them yourself is pleasant.

So potent was religion in persuading to evil deeds.

We are each of us angels with only one wing, and we can only fly by embracing one another.

-- Lucretius (96 BC - 55 BC)

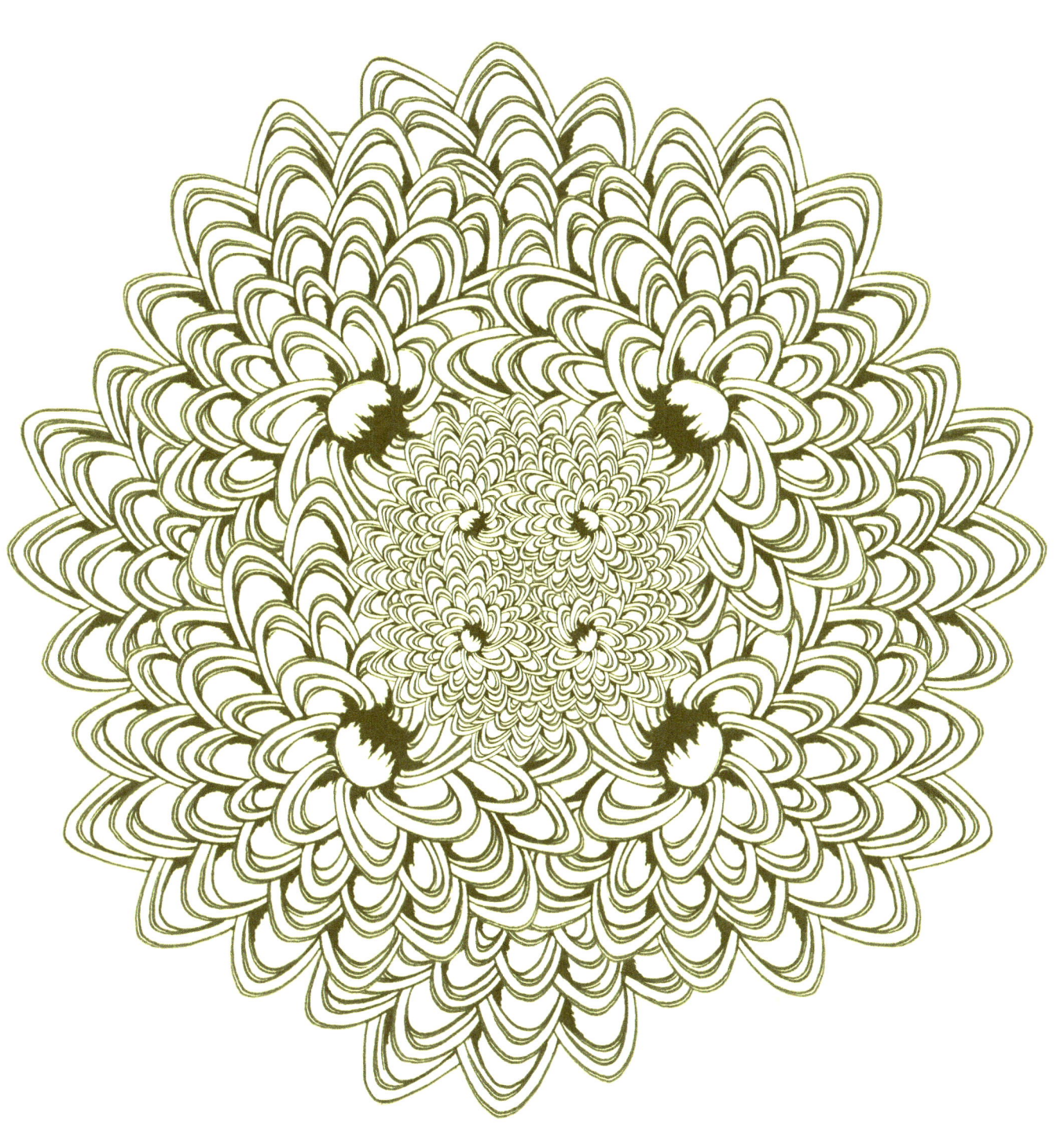

For it would have been better that man should have been born dumb, nay, void of all reason, rather than that he should employ the gifts of Providence to the destruction of his neighbor.

It is much easier to try one's hand at many things than to concentrate one's powers on one thing.

-- Marcus Fabius Quintilian (35 – 90 AD)

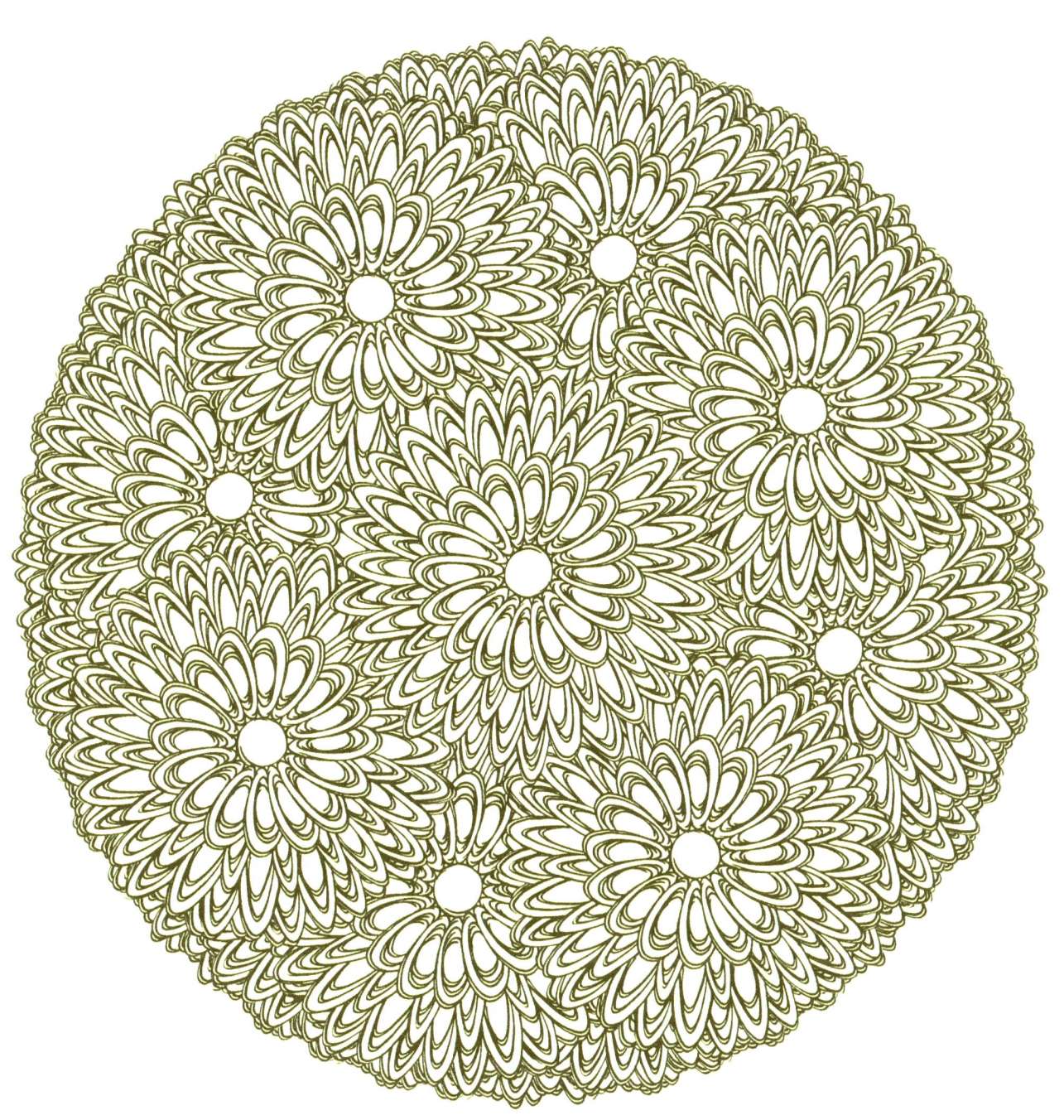

Adapt yourself to the things among which your lot has been cast and love sincerely the fellow creatures with whom destiny has ordained that you shall live.

Be content with what you are, and wish not change; nor dread your last day, nor long for it.

To refrain from imitation is the best revenge.

-- Marcus Aurelius (121 – 180 AD)

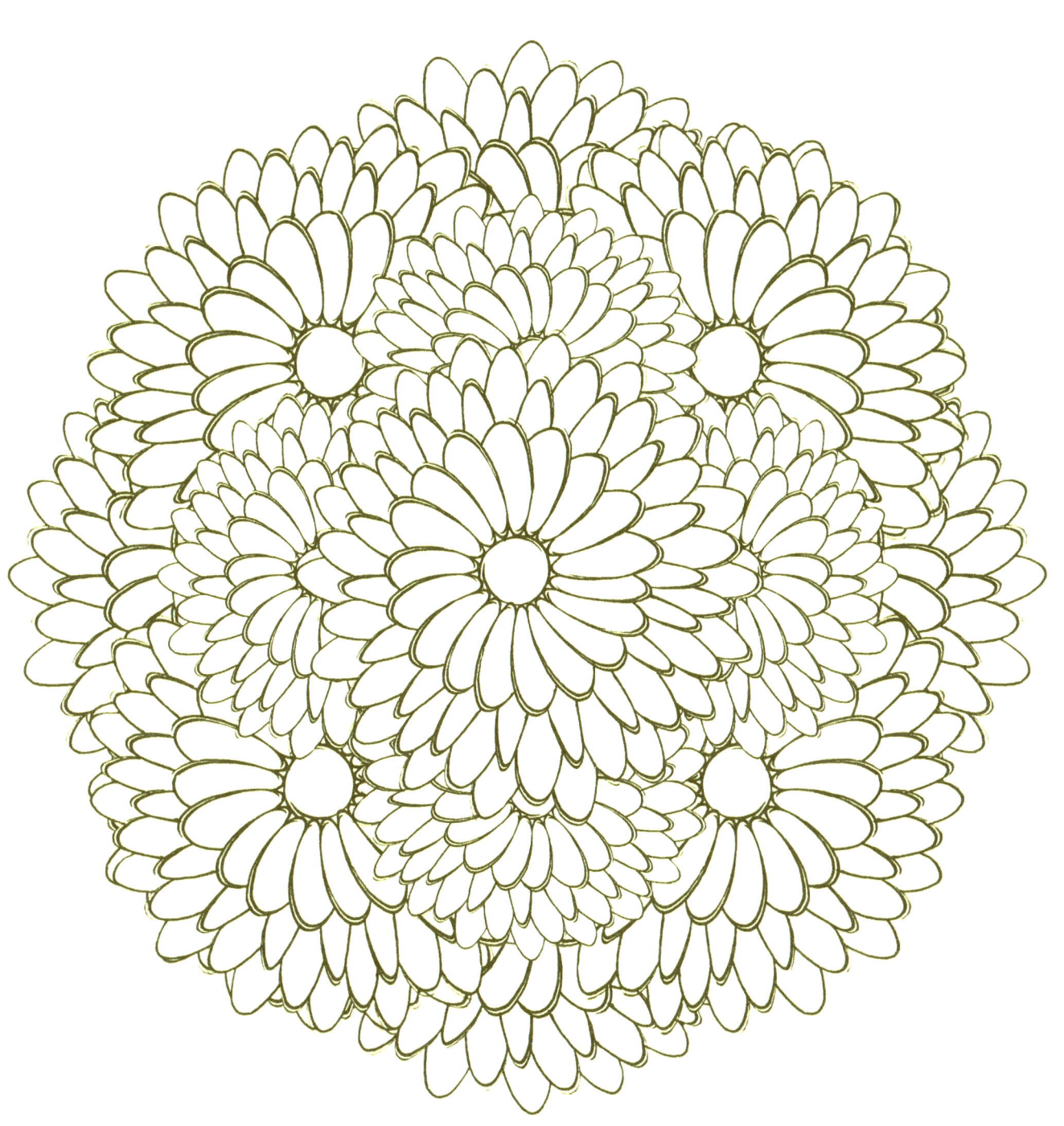

Do thou restrain the haughty spirit in thy breast, for better far is gentle courtesy.

A councilor ought not to sleep the whole night through, a man to whom the populace is entrusted, and who has many responsibilities.

The difficulty is not so great to die for a friend, as to find a friend worth dying for.

A sympathetic friend can be quite as dear as a brother.

-- Homer (8ᵗʰ Century BC)

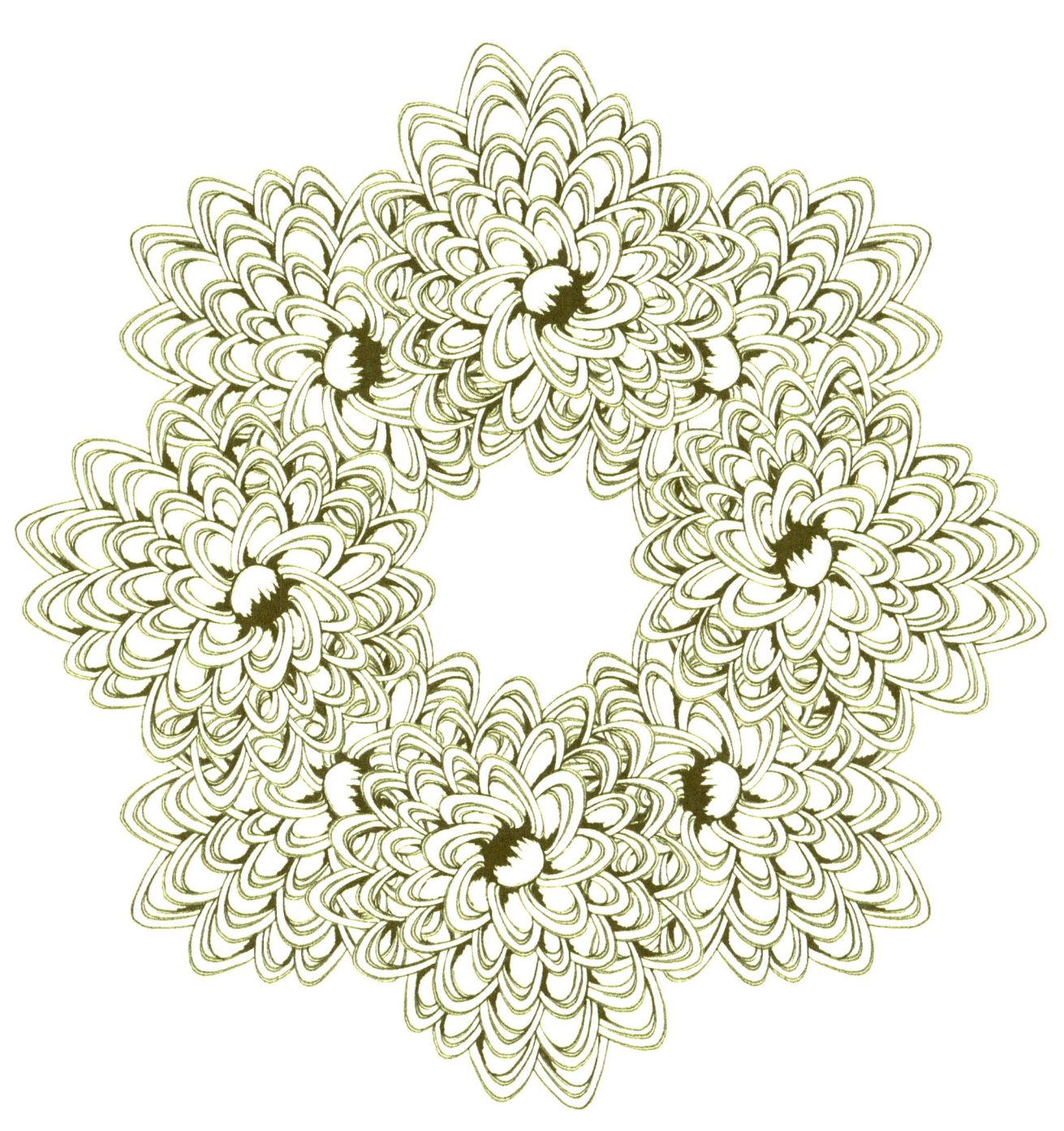

The wise learn many things from their foes.

Wise men, though all laws were abolished, would lead the same lives.

-- Aristophanes (450 BC - 385 BC)

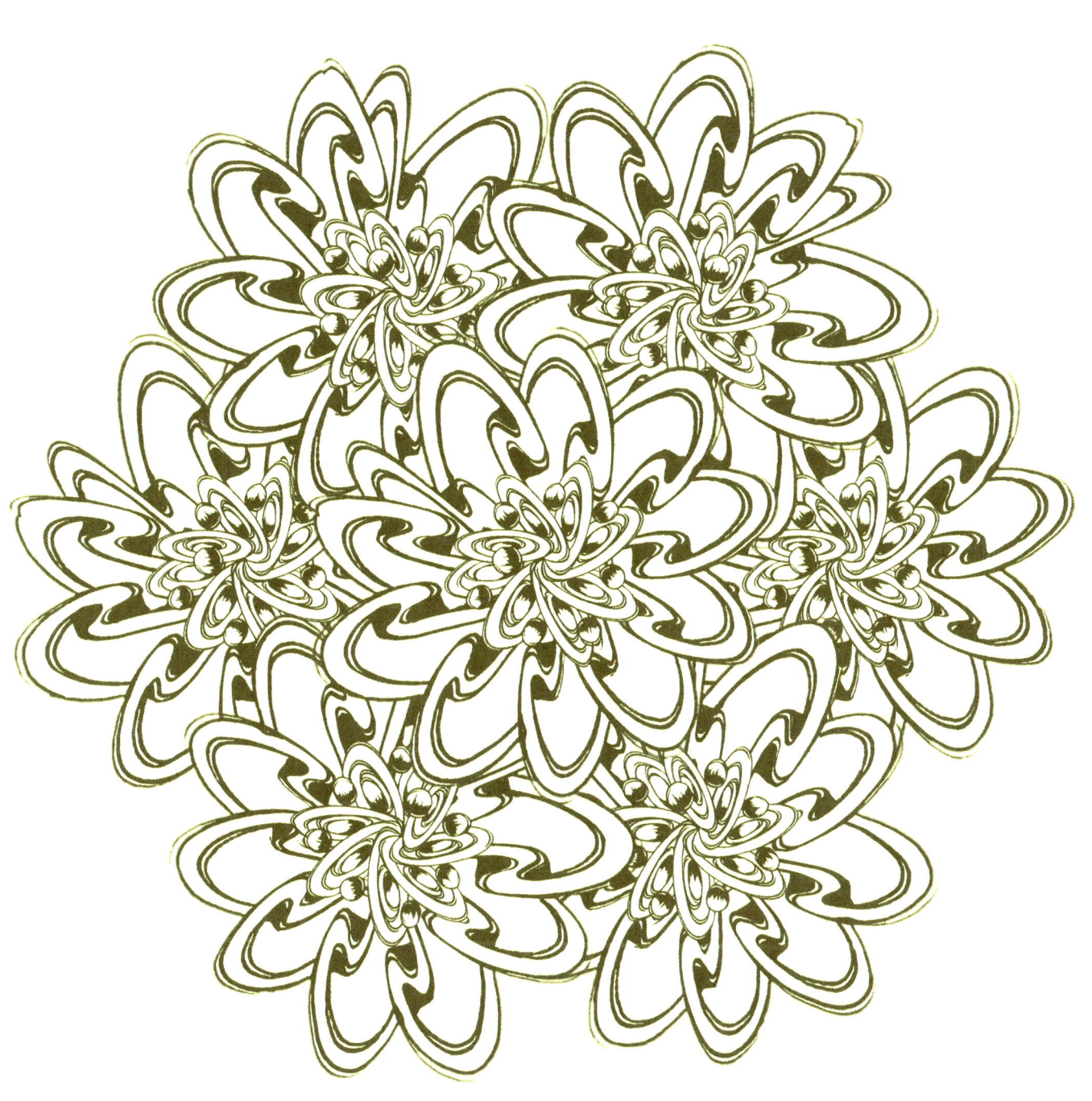

Begin, be bold and venture to be wise.

Clogged with yesterday's excess, the body drags the mind down with it.

He who postpones the hour of living rightly is like the rustic who waits for the river to run out before he crosses.

*-- **Horace (65 - 8 BC)***

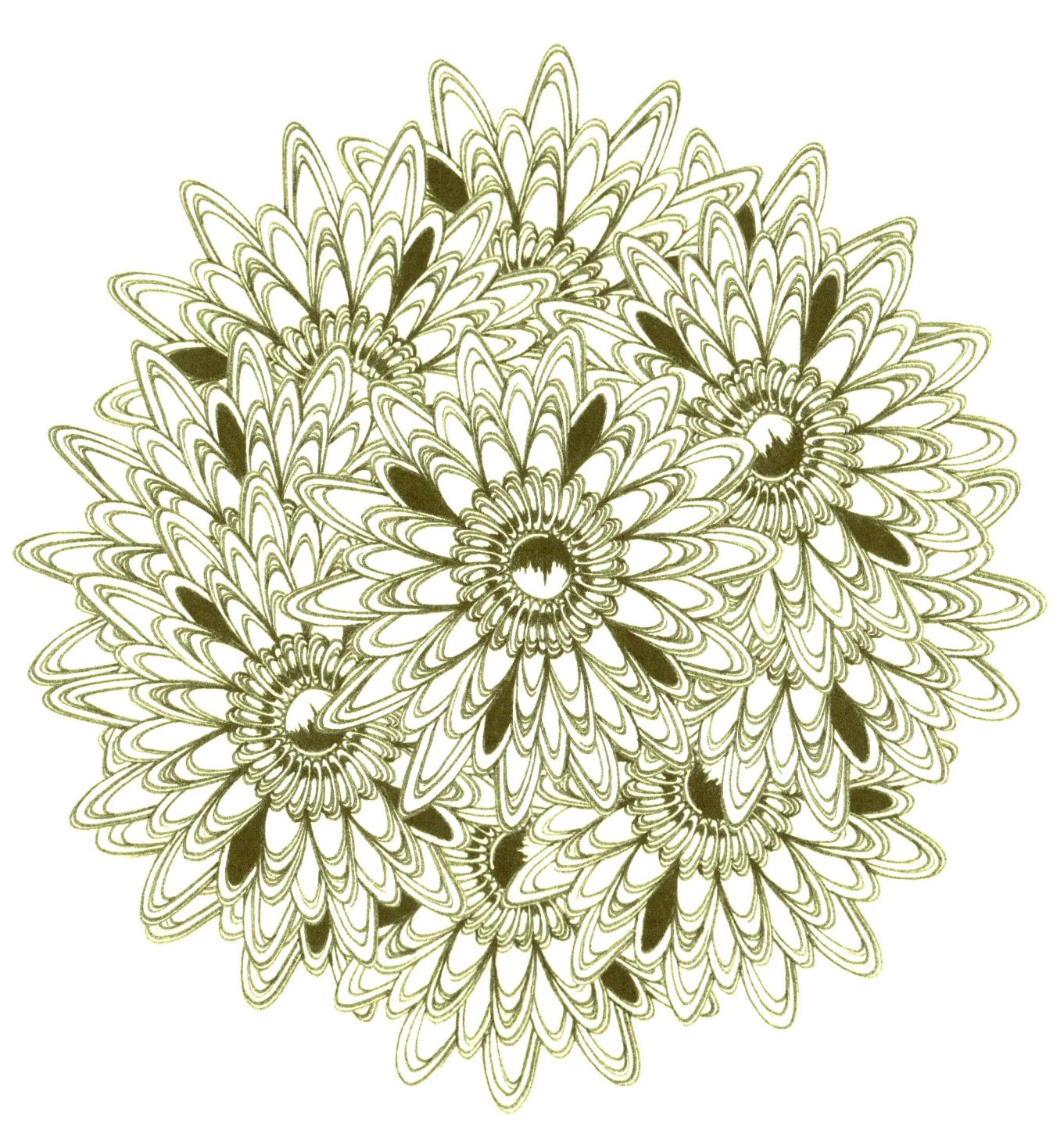

The oldest, shortest words - "yes" and "no" - are those which require the most thought.

It is better wither to be silent, or to say things of more value than silence. Sooner throw a pearl at hazard than an idle or useless word; and do not say a little in many words, but a great deal in a few.

Friends are as companions on a journey, who ought to aid each other to persevere in the road to a happier life.

It is only necessary to make war with five things; with the maladies of the body, the ignorance of the mind, with the passions of the body, with the seditions of the city and the discords of families.

-- Pythagoras (582 BC – 497 BC)

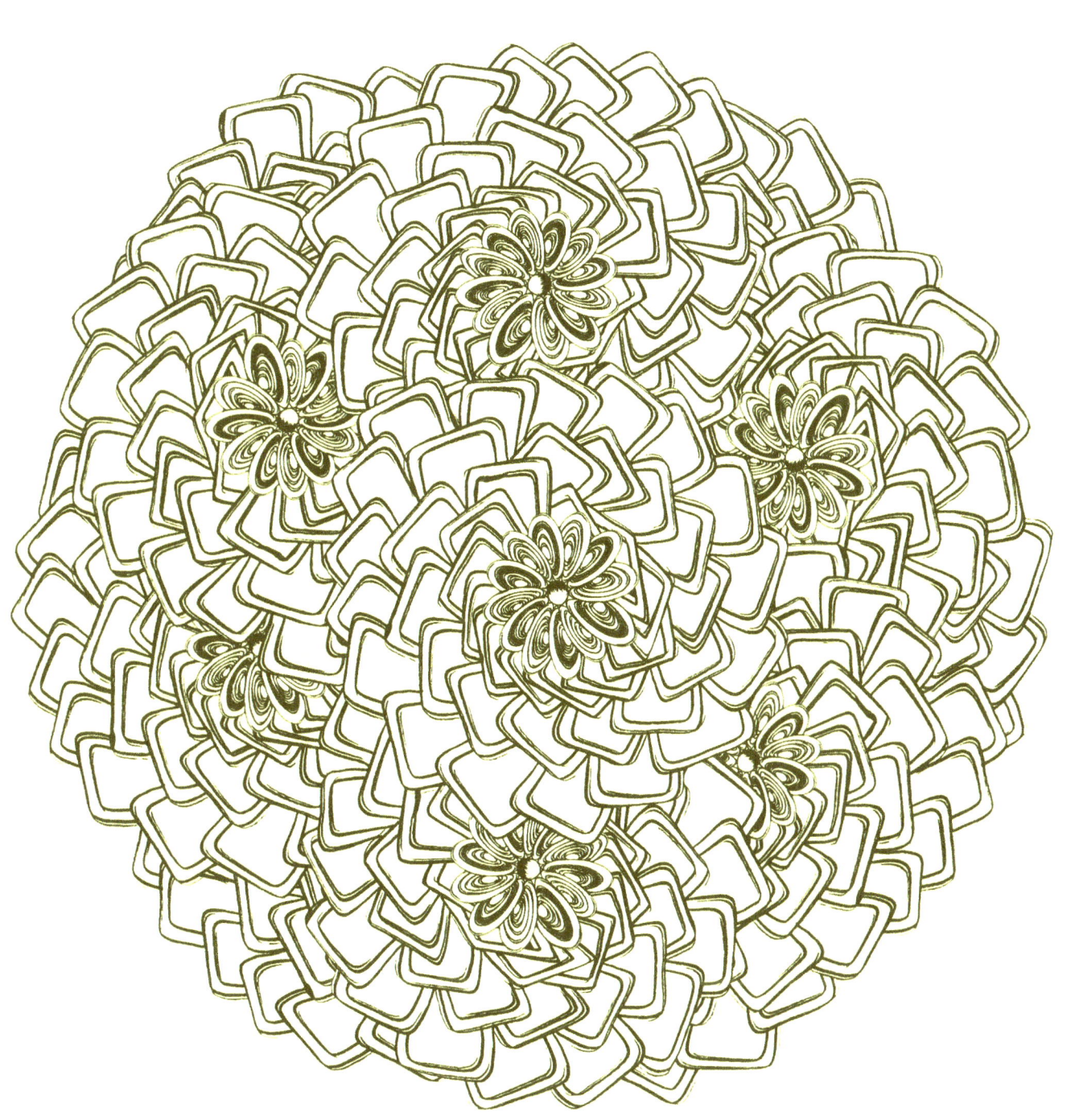

Fill your bowl to the brim and it will spill.
Keep sharpening your knife and it will blunt.

Govern a great nation as you would cook a
small fish. Do not overdo it.

He who controls others may be powerful, but he
who has mastered himself is mightier still.

-- Lao Tzu (604 BC - 531 BC)

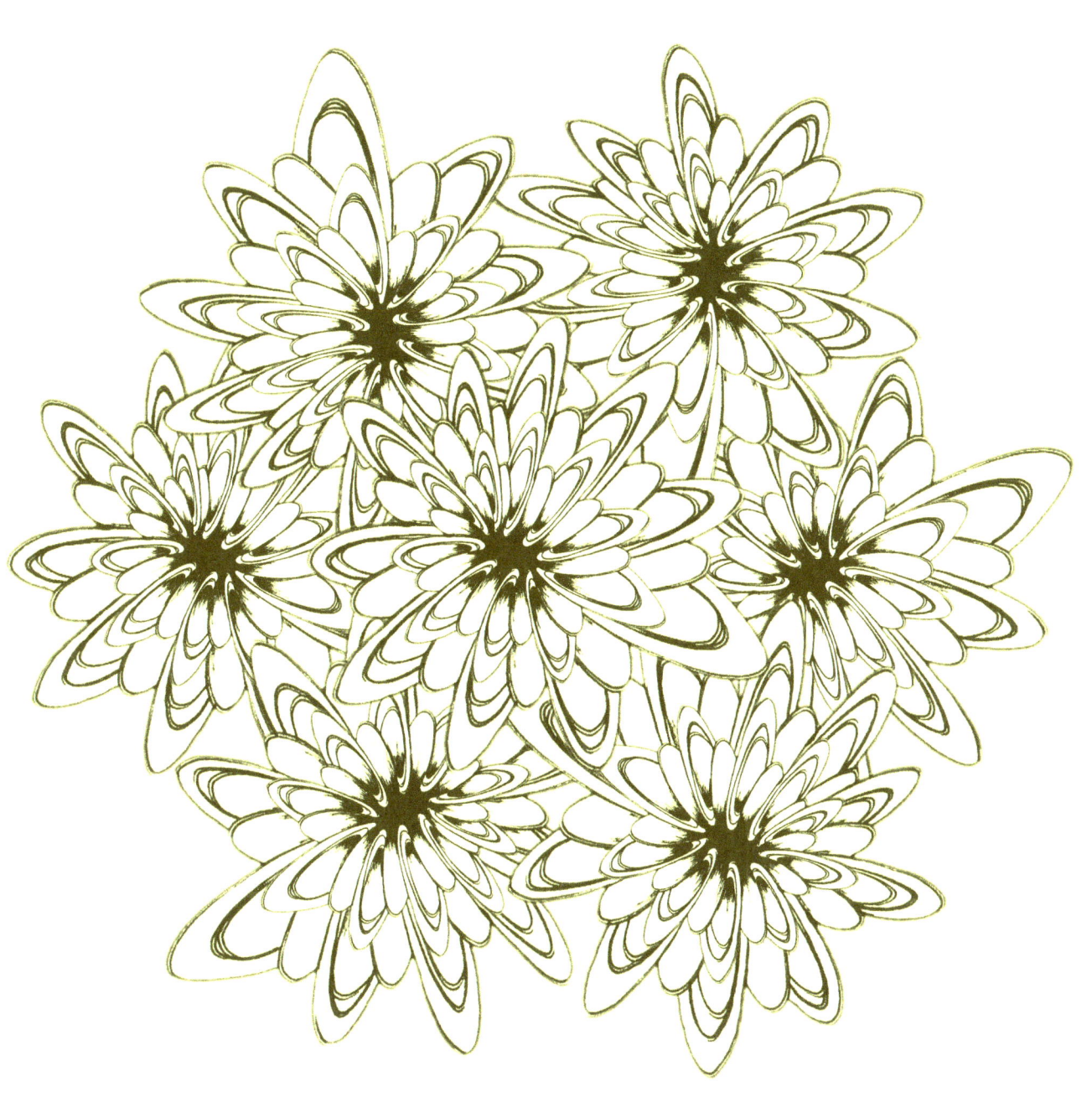

Alas, how quickly the gratitude owed to the dead flows off, how quick to be proved a deceiver.

The greatest grieves are those we cause ourselves.

The soul that has conceived one's wickedness can nurse no good thereafter.

-- Sophocles (496 BC - 406 BC)

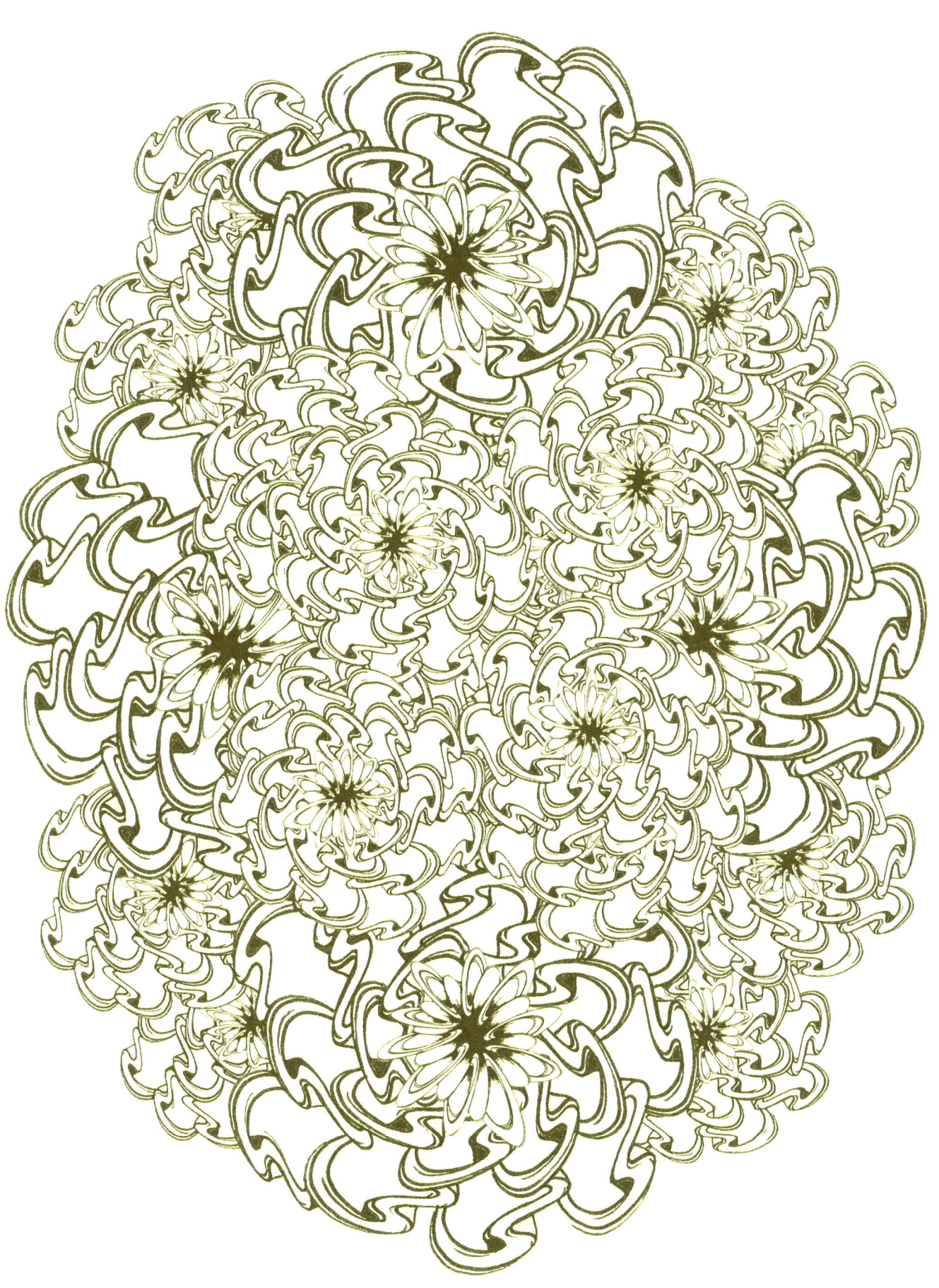

It were better to have no opinion of God at all than such a one as is unworthy of him; for the one is only belief - the other contempt.

Let us carefully observe those good qualities wherein our enemies excel us; and endeavor to excel them, by avoiding what is faulty, and imitating what is excellent in them.

*-- **Plutarch (46 – 120 AD)***

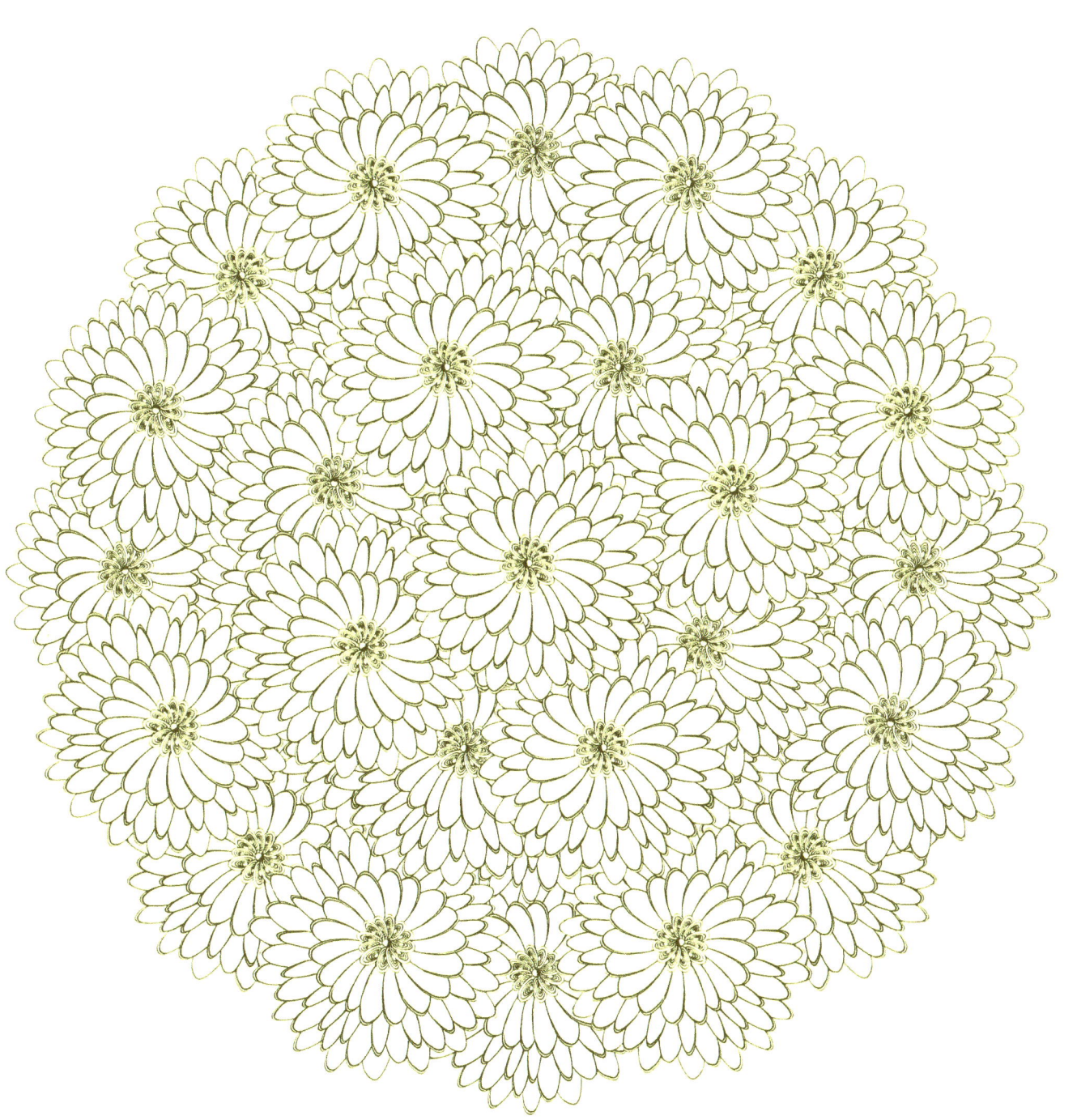

The Impossible is Infinite.

-- Argo Ink (1964 – present)

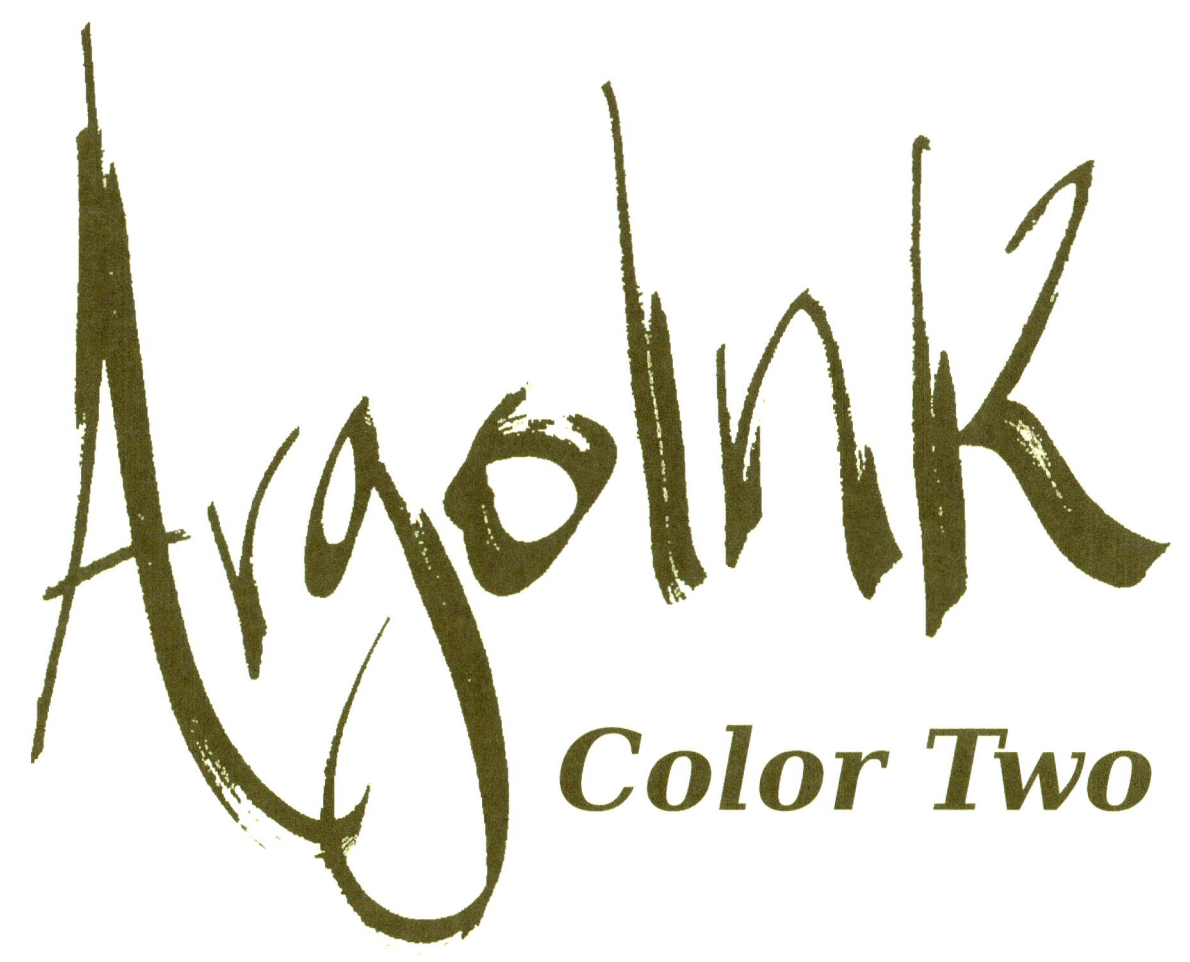

Color Two

All ArgoInk products are available at 50% off their normal retail price when purchased for school and charitable fundraising events.

Please visit our web site for more details.

www.ArgoInk.com